the George W. Bush
COLORING BOOK

Copyright © 2004 Garrett County Press

For more information address:
GARRETT COUNTY PRESS, LLC
828 Royal St. #248
New Orleans, LA 70116
www.gcpress.com

Garrett County Press First Edition 2004 (XB238TT-6)

ISBN: 1-891053-94-9

Illustrations and Design by Karen A. Ocker

KAREN OCKER DESIGN designkorp@earthlink.net
Karen Ocker (*Art Director, Book Designer, Illustrator, Painter*) earned her degree in Graphic Design from the School of Visual Arts-New York City, where she worked as a freelance graphic designer and artist for 17 years. She has worked on countless promotional, marketing and advertising projects for local businesses, not-for-profits and national corporations. She has designed more than 100 book covers and interiors for publishers including: Random House, Pearson Publishing, Tuttle Publishing, John Wiley & Sons, Garrett County Press and more. This is her first coloring book.

FOOTNOTE ON BUSH BY JOLEY WOOD
Joley Wood (*Editor-in-Chief,* Garrett County Press) is a graduate with a degree in English from the University of Wisconsin—Madison, where he read a lot of and did theses on comics and Irish literature. He worked as a teacher's aid and wrote local television ads before moving to Ireland, where he completed a M. Phil in Anglo-Irish literature and worked as an English language teacher, among other things. He has written on numerous Irish writers, including essays on James Joyce, George Bernard Shaw and William Butler Yeats, and a preface for Shaw's Saint Joan. Twentieth century Irish writing has just as much social realism as Temp Slave! and C.S. Walton's work on Russia, which makes him a conveniently knowledgeable yet pleasantly indifferent editor.

the George W. Bush
COLORING BOOK

illustrated by
Karen A. Ocker

With a historical footnote by
Joley Wood

GARRETT COUNTY PRESS

Dedicated to Debra Forfreedom

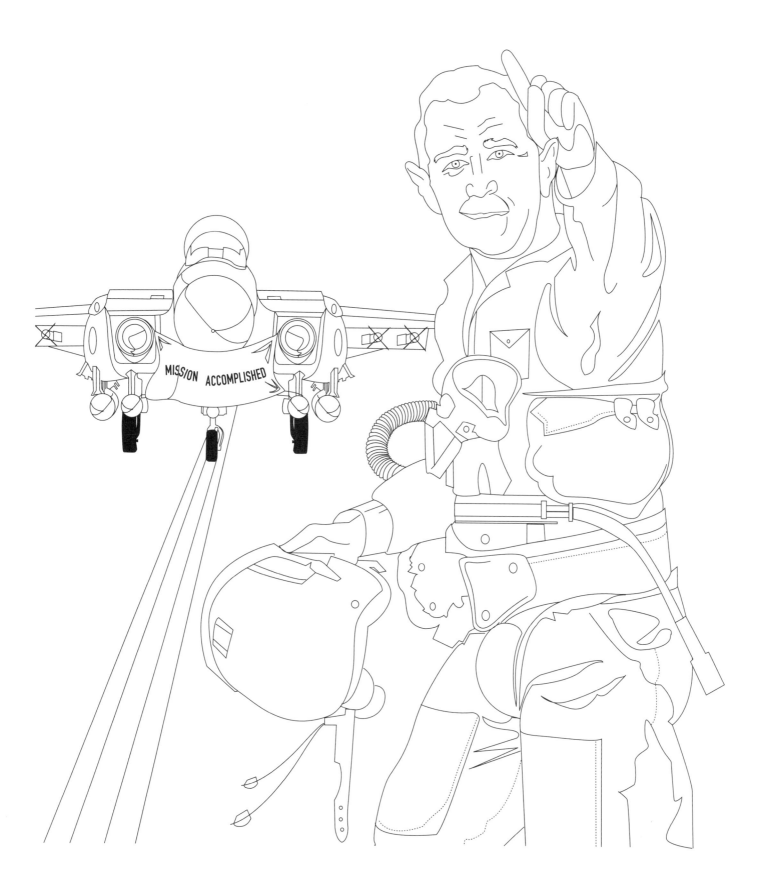

"First, let me make it very clear, poor people aren't necessarily killers. Just because you happen to be not rich doesn't mean you're willing to kill."

—Washington, D.C., May 19, 2003

"They [Democrats] want the federal government controlling
Social Security like it's some kind of federal program..."

—Campaign Rally, November 02, 2000

"I was raised in the West. The west of Texas. It's pretty close to California.
In more ways than Washington, D.C., is close to California."

—on a trip to California, April 8, 2000

'The fundamental question is, 'Will I be a successful president when it comes to foreign policy?' I will be. But until I'm the president, it's going to be hard for me to verify that I think I'll be more effective."

—Wayne, Michigan, June 27, 2000

"People say, how can I help on this war against terror? How can I fight evil? You can do so by mentoring a child; by going into a shut-in's house and say I love you..."

—Washington, D.C., September 19, 2002

"There's only one person who hugs the mothers and the widows, the wives and the kids upon the death of their loved one. Others hug but having committed the troops, I've got an additional responsibility to hug and that's me and I know what it's like."

—on 20/20 December 2002

"...we must not allow the world's worst leaders to develop and harbor the world's worst weapons. I got a lot of tools at my disposal, and I'm a patient man; and I'm a patient man."

—Oklahoma City, Oklahoma, August 29, 2002

9 •   •10

8 •   •11
                •5   •4

                                    3 •
7 •   •6
                                            •12

2 •

                        •13

1 •————————————————• 14

1 •————————————————• 4

2 •   •3

"It's amazing I won. I was running against peace, prosperity and incumbency."

—speaking to Swedish Prime Minister Goran Perrson, June 14, 2001

"I know the human being and the fish can coexist peacefully."

—Bush discussing fisheries issues in Michigan. Date unknown.

"We spent a lot of time talking about Africa, and we should.
Africa is a nation that suffers from incredible disease."

—Goteborg, Sweden, June 14, 2001

"Let me put it to you that way. Conservation is important. That's going to be an important ingredient . . . but we need energy. The California crunch really is the result of not enough power-generating plants and then not enough power to power the power of generating plants."

—at his ranch in Crawford, Texas, January 12, 2001

"Redefining the role of the United States from enablers to keep the peace
to enablers to keep the peace from the peacekeepers is going to be an assignment."

—at his ranch in Crawford, Texas, January 12, 2001

"Nobody wishes this evil had ever happened, but as a result of evil there are some amazing things that are taking place in America."

—Daytona, Florida, January 30, 2002

"We need an energy bill that encourages consumption..."

—Trenton, New Jersey, September 23, 2002

"I don't remember debates. I don't think we spent a lot of time debating it [The Vietnam War]. Maybe we did, but I don't remember."

—July 27, 1999

"Do you have blacks, too?"

—Washington D.C., November 8, 2001
Question posed from Bush to President Fernando Henrique Cardoso of Brazil

"All in all, it's been a fabulous year for Laura and me."

—Washington D.C., December 22, 2001

QUOTE SOURCE NOTES

1. "First let me make it clear . . . "
Recorded at a news conference held with Philippine President Arroyo on May 19, 2003.
SOURCE: *Federal Document Clearing House Inc.*

2. "They want the federal government controlling the Social Security like . . . "
National Public Radio's *"All Things Considered"* (November 2, 2000) reported Bush's observation from the Family Arena in St. Charles, Missouri. In this instance he was arguing for his proposal to let young people invest their Social Security taxes in the stock market.

3. "I was raised in the West . . . "
Cathleen Decker reported this quote in a *LA Times* piece that appeared on April 8, 2000 headlined, *"Bush Courts Latinos, Other Californians"*

4. "The fundamental question is, 'Will I be a successful president . . . '"
He uttered these words at a news conference in Wayne, Michigan. Bush was appearing with Michigan Governor, John Engler.
SOURCE: *New York Times* (June 28, 2000).

5. "People say, how can I help on this war against . . . "
This quote ends with the slightly salacious, ". . . If you're interested in helping America fight evil, love your neighbor just like you'd like to be loved yourself." Spoken at the Republican Governors Association Fall Reception at the National Building Museum.
SOURCE: *Federal Document Clearing House Inc.* (September 19, 2002)

6. "There's only one person who hugs the mothers and the widows . . . "
Both the *Toronto Star Newspaper* and *Anchorage Daily News* (December 29, 2002) reported that Bush made this remark in a December 13, 2001 interview with Barbara Walters. The *Toronto Star* referenced the quote in itsentertainment section in a short piece about the *"F*ck George Bush Film Festival"* that was being held at the University of Toronto's Innis College.

7. "We must not allow the world's worst leaders . . . "
Uttered in Oklahoma City, Oklahoma at a "Largent for Governor and Ihofe for Senate Luncheon."
SOURCE: *Federal Document Clearing House Inc.* (August 29, 2002)

8. "It was amazing I won. I was running against peace and prosperity and incumbency."
The *New York Times* reported in a June 16, 2001 piece by Frank Bruni that a Swedish television crew picked up the aside as Bush was joking with Swedish Prime Minister, Goran Persson.

9. "I know the human being and fish can coexist . . . "
"I actually said this 'I know the human being and fish can coexist peacefully.'

Now, that makes you stop and think. Anyone can give you a coherent sentence, but something like this takes you into an entirely new dimension," Bush said.
SOURCE: *The Washington Times* (March 31, 2001)

10. "We spent a lot of time talking about Africa . . . "
This particularly embarrassing display of geographical understanding was displayed at Bush's first European Union meeting. *The New York Times* reported in a June 15, 2001 story by Frank Bruni that European leaders and Bush disagreed on just about everything. Arguments flared over Bush's missile shield plan, the Kyoto Protocol and—incredibly—the expansion of the European Union. "My vision of Europe is a larger vision," Bush said.

11. "Let me put it to you that way. Conservation is . . . "
Plenty of great Bushisms came out of this interview with *The New York Times* that took place on his ranch in Crawford, Texas. The interview was conducted on January 12, 2002 and appeared in the January 14th Sunday edition.

12. "Redefining the role of the United States . . . "
Also from his January 12, 2001 Crawford sit-down with the *New York Times*.

13. "Nobody wishes this evil . . . "
According to the *Federal News Service Inc.* this was spoken at a "FLORIDA WELCOME CEREMONY" on January 30, 2002. He went on to say, "People have really begun to challenge the culture of the past that said, 'If it feels good, do it,' to welcome a new culture that says, 'I'm responsible for the decisions I make in life.'"

14. "We need an energy bill that encourages consumption."
This Energy Bill speech was delivered at a National Guard base in Trenton, NJ.
SOURCE: *Federal News Service, Inc.* (September 23, 2002)

15. "I don't remember debates . . . "
Evidently, Bush never debated the merits of the Vietnam War while he was an undergraduate at Yale.
SOURCE: *Washington Post* (August 1, 1999)

16. "Do you have blacks, too?"
This was an off-the-record bit of conversation picked up between Bush and President Fernando Henrique Cardoso of Brazil. The social blunder was widely reported abroad.
SOURCE: *Der Spiegal* (May 19, 2002)

17, "All in all, it's been a fabulous year for Laura and me."
Mike Allen reported this untimely observation in a December 22, 2001 *Washington Post* piece about the war on terrorism. "The presidency might be a burden in these times, but it seemed to rest lightly for at least a day," Allen wrote.

A HISTORICAL FOOTNOTE BY JOLEY WOOD

Bush (bŏŏsh) NOUN: **1.** A low shrub with many branches. **2.** A thick growth of shrubs; a thicket. **3a.** Land covered with dense vegetation or undergrowth. **b.** Land remote from settlement: the *Australian bush.* **4a.** A shaggy mass, as of hair. **b.** *Vulgar Slang* A growth of pubic hair. **5.** A fox's tail. **6a.** *Archaic* A clump of ivy hung outside a tavern to indicate the availability of wine inside. **b.** *Obsolete* A tavern. (*American Heritage Dictionary*)

Anyone who knows how to use a coloring book knows our leaders lie to us, but the mark of the 21st century leader will be the person who gets others to believe the lie even when they know it's a lie. And George W. Bush has mastered this rhetorical mojo — even the press falls for it. This administration has so altered the face of the U.S. presidency and the Republican party that even Kevin Phillips, author of 1969's *The Emerging Republican Majority* and from that major advisor to the Nixon administration, has swapped his Republican card for independent status and wrote a recent book about how the Bush's have changed U.S. governance into the kind of dynastic thing we once fought a revolution over (*American Dynasty*). But let's understand something here: No one doubts this guy was appointed by the Supreme Court, not elected by the people, and anyone who wants to argue that Bush really did win Florida has to explain the whole Database Technologies International ignomiy. For those not in the know (which by the U.S. coverage is most of us), Database Technologies International was hired by then Florida Secretary of State Katherine Harris and Gov. Jeb Bush to come up with a list of felons to be purged from the Florida voting rolls, and the company has admitted they wrongfully purged over 90,000 voters for the 2000 election, primarily from Black American counties and districts. This in an election decided by just over 500 votes, an election that may prove one of the most significant in the history of democratic nations. Database Technologies International admitted all this, but it only made the foreign papers, not here where we needed to put our long national nightmare to rest. Is the nightmare over? Some just know Bush is the best president ever and don't need anything like news or facts to tell them what's what (much like our president has admitted), while others like to note that we live in a republic, not a democracy, where the people elect representatives to speak the public's mind, so the popular vote doesn't really matter. But this administration even leaves a lot to be desired on the representation front. First, less than 50% of the U.S. electorate voted in the 2000 election. The (counted) votes were split 50/50, which means only about 23% of the electorate voted for this president. That's nowhere close to a mandate, even if he or anyone really does think the Almighty appointed him. And the administration's messianic zeal in its own rightness has meant such wacky policies as (1.) **Withdrawing from global environmental standards:** Kyoto. (2.) **Turning over the right to pollute to corporations:** Industries like the energy industry are now allotted a certain measure of allowable pollutants, like poker chips, and can now buy the rights to pollute from other companies who aren't using up their own pollution poker chips. (3.) **Trying to stack the courts with right-wing ideologues:** As I write this Charles Pickering, who is famous for supporting the rights of people to burn crosses in protest of black people's, well, right to exist, has just been installed on the

New Orleans 5th Circuit Court of Appeals by Bush over the protests of Congress. (4.) **The stonewalling of the public's right to information:** Late on a Wednesday night in early November, 2001 Bush passed an executive order effectively sealing all presidential records and overturning the Freedom of Information Act by putting the onus on the individual to prove in court, at one's own expense, why those records should be made available. The FOIA had been around since the Kennedy assassination in 1966 and was expanded after Watergate, and now after 9/11, when such records could be *really fucking important*, the act might as well be in the grave with JFK or Nixon. (5.) **The crushing of public education:** Standardized testing? Anyone who knows anything about education knows that standardized testing only tests *how well one can take a test*, not real knowledge. That's why people take courses to beat the SAT, the GRE, the LSAT or the MCAT. The insidious thing is if students don't perform up to the test's standards (incidentally established in company boardrooms, not by educators), those public schools lose funding. Do you see the logic in this? Think about some of the worst cases — Chicago Public Schools, Milwaukee Public Schools, L.A. or New York or really any U.S. public school in a city, schools with overcrowded classrooms, a dearth of outdated books, leaking ceilings and broken windows: the economics behind the funding of schools dictates the quality of a student's education, and if those students who need the most help don't fill in the right blank on a standardized test, they lose their meager funding, or even their school. If we had the teachers and the cojones we'd be doing something useful like comprehensive testing. (6.) **The loss of support by our international allies:** After 9/11 even the French offered to send some military aid to Afghanistan, and we gave them a big finger. We did things our way: we secured the country long enough to set up a pipeline leading from the Caspian Sea to a failing power plant in North India owned by (guess who?) Enron and Ken Lay. Dick Cheney had been lobbying for that while he was still the titular head of Halliburton … who says tragedy and opportunism don't mix? Also recall that next to no one here covered the story that the U.S. was tapping the phones and hacking the computers of Cameroon, Mexico, Angola, Pakistan, Chile, Bulgaria and Guinea at the United Nations when it was looking to build its "Coalition of the Willing." Our relations with Mexico markedly cooled around this time. Is this any way to garner international support, by spying on possible allies? The 28-year-old staffer at the British Government Communications Headquarters who leaked this information to the *London Observer* newspaper has now been arrested for her act. (7.) **And of course the first overt imperial invasion of another country in modern U.S. history:** Ignore pre-modern military wars, where more blood on hands and no computers made things more complicated. And at least Lyndon Johnson could reasonably claim to be duped by the Pentagon with the Gulf of Tonkin incident. There's more evidence that this administration ordered selectively shaped evidence to justify an invasion than there is of any chemical, biological or nuclear weapons in Iraq. Nice how they then blamed faulty intelligence when they found squat for WMD. Bush's former Secretary of the Treasury, Paul O'Neill, has released documents of meetings from his time in the cabinet, and at the top of the list at the first meeting was how to invade Iraq — just read *Wall Street Journal* reporter Ron Suskind's new book on O'Neill, *The Price of Loyalty* (O'Neill is of course now being investigated by the administration). The documentary evidence that Iraq was getting uranium from Niger? Forged. How about those imminent and dangerous Iraqi ties to Al Qaeda? Also nonexistent. The presence of all those weapons dumps Colin Powell showed off to the U.N.? Nonexistent. The Carnegie Endowment for International Peace published a study in January, 2004 showing that none of the claims from Powell's famous U.N. speech have proven true; and don't forget what happened just hours after the news broke that one of the reports used was plagiarized from a grad student's thesis written in the early 1990's — we went to orange alert, and that dominated the headlines for the next week, shoving plagiarism past our short attention spans. Not even the Jessica Lynch story was true, and she showed real heroism by denying the lies and withdrawing from the patriotic patronage (let's hear it for working class values). But damn were we daft … In September 2003 the *Washington Post* published a poll showing that nearly 70% of the U.S. public believed Iraq had something to do with 9/11. Who could blame them, when even as late as January 2004, administration advisor Richard Perle was still pronouncing that 9/11 changed everything and demanded Iraq's invasion? This is called an enthymematic argument — you state two things next to each other without actually linking them in order to suggest the link without taking responsibility for it. Perle's great at this, and it makes him as slippery as a fish. But when Perle pisses on your leg and tells you it's raining, we seem to sense it, yet Bush appears so disconnected there's almost no feeling to sense, and that's where we misunderestimate him. (He warned us about that.) Of course if we were actually reading past the splashy headlines we might have known. We might had read the end of defense analyst William Arkin's October 27, 2002 *L.A. Times* article noting Rumsfeld's joint CIA-military group called P2OG, Proactive Preemptive Operations Group; their mandate is to "stimulate reactions" among terrorist groups so U.S. forces can react and attack. *THIS MEANS THEY'RE HELPING TO CREATE TERRORIST ACTIVITY SO WE CAN ATTACK TERRORISTS AND IF THAT DOESN'T SCARE THE HELL OUT OF YOU IT SHOULD AT LEAST GIVE YOU THE HEEBEEJEEBEES.* There's an illogical short-circuit between fighting a war on terror and fomenting terrorist activity that's not being addressed in this country. P2OG was of great interest to some of the press — the *Moscow Times*, the *Asia Times*, the British press and *UPI*, and even *ABC News* for a little while, but really no where else in the U.S. Someone needs to shout IF WE'RE IN A WAR ON TERRORISM, WHY ARE WE TRYING TO STIMULATE TERRORIST ACTIVITY? WHO'S FLYING THIS PLANE? I leave the morality of this position for the reader to wrestle with. On morality: It turns out those energy contact meetings of Cheney's to determine U.S. energy policy, those meetings whose minutes were subpoenaed by the General Accounting Office through three years of Vice Presidential stonewalling, show that long before 9/11 these groups had certain interests in Iraqi oil fields — the subpoenaed documents have maps. And it's no secret that Cheney's old company is profiting healthily off rebuilding Iraq for a second time in a decade. It's no secret that Perle and Henry Kissinger (who was slated to head the 9/11 investigation commission) sit on the boards of venture capital firms like Trireme Partners LP in New York, who are profiting healthily on the new Middle Eastern mess through partnerships with defense contractors like Boeing. Let's remember Perle sits on and once chaired the Defense Policy Board and as such was the buzz in Donald Rumsfeld's ear; at the same time Trireme stood to gain $20 million from a Boeing deal if the Pentagon leased a certain Boeing tanker. In other words, as long as we went to war, this deal went through. So far nothing has got in this administration's way, not the press, and not even the facts — we still don't know who leaked CIA agent Valerie Plame's name to Robert Novak after her husband's intelligence report showed the Niger uranium claim was false, we still haven't seen the documents subpoenaed by the 9/11 commission (and Speaker of the House Dennis Hastert is now taking steps to make sure the commission never gets those documents), and we're hearing hardly anything about those soldiers injured (we know over 500 U.S. soldiers have been killed, but *Time* and the *London Independ*ent have reported that to date over 1,500 have suffered battle casualties, and over 9,000 other soldiers have been flown out and hospitalized … and that's just the U.S. side). But if more proof were needed that there weren't any real threats demanding this real war, look no further than the initial push into Iraq, then go down to your local VFW for a beer and a chat with a vet about this. We were told Iraq had and may use biological or chemical weapons on our troops. If there were such weapons in Iraq, or worse, and Rumsfeld sent in troops as thinly as he did, with unsupported supply lines and no back-up, imagine for a second what would have happened if they were attacked with a weapon of mass destruction; how would the supply lines get reestablished? Who would bring in the medical supplies? Who would offer back-up support? Who would carry out the injured and secure the area? What troops were there would be decimated, and Rumsfeld would be looking for a new job. The only way to justify sending in troops so thin is if they knew there were in reality no such threats. Of course, then you get things like mechanics and cooks and supply clerks doing the fighting, not the trained infantry who are supposed to secure their lines. Of course that's exactly what happened. Nice how this also helped their pending tax cut; remember how it was Wisconsin's Russ Feingold who noted that we needed tax dollars to support our troops, so we couldn't give all the tax cut Bush was asking for. Now imagine if there was a real threat and we had to send in the amount of troops the generals were calling for; there would have been next to no tax cut. Let's put it together: construction and defense contracts, designs on oil fields, a way to scare the public into some kind of ordered discipline through color-coded brain-games, and those who are already profiting on that side of the coin get a little scratch through the back pocket when we're looking East messing ourselves about imagined threats. Human life has just been set to the dollar standard, and people have become meat to be traded. And what were we told to do? Go shopping….

There was a 1960's British television show called *The Prisoner.* A secret agent resigns and is kidnapped to an island of people who know too much — their every need and comfort is provided, yet they can never leave. Everyone is given a number, and our hero is Number Six. Each episode has a new Number Two who runs the island and is set with the mission of breaking Number Six and finding out why he resigned. Every time Number Six tries to escape a roving blob sucks him in and drags him back, and these attempts are given different emergency codes — Code Yellow, Code Orange, Code Red (coincidentally the same codes our Department of Homeland Security uses — maybe Tom Ridge was a fan.) Every episode begins with Number Six asking "Who is Number One," and Number Two always responds, "You are Number Six." Is Number Two just saying that our hero is called Number Six, or is Number Two saying "You are (Number One), Number Six." We are now in the same position as Number Six and don't realize it. There is a jihad on our shores, it's just coming from Pennsylvania Avenue, and if we really believe this is a democracy, or even a republic and not an oligarchy, we need to realize we have the power and ability to alter things — it's just going to take more than 23% of us if we don't want to be prisoners of our own design. But if we allow our Number Two's to get us to believe the lies when we know they're lies, we'll have little choice in the matter.